PSYCHIATRIST

COLORING BOOK

THIS BOOK BELONGS TO:

....

One Patient
away
From
Becoming a
patient

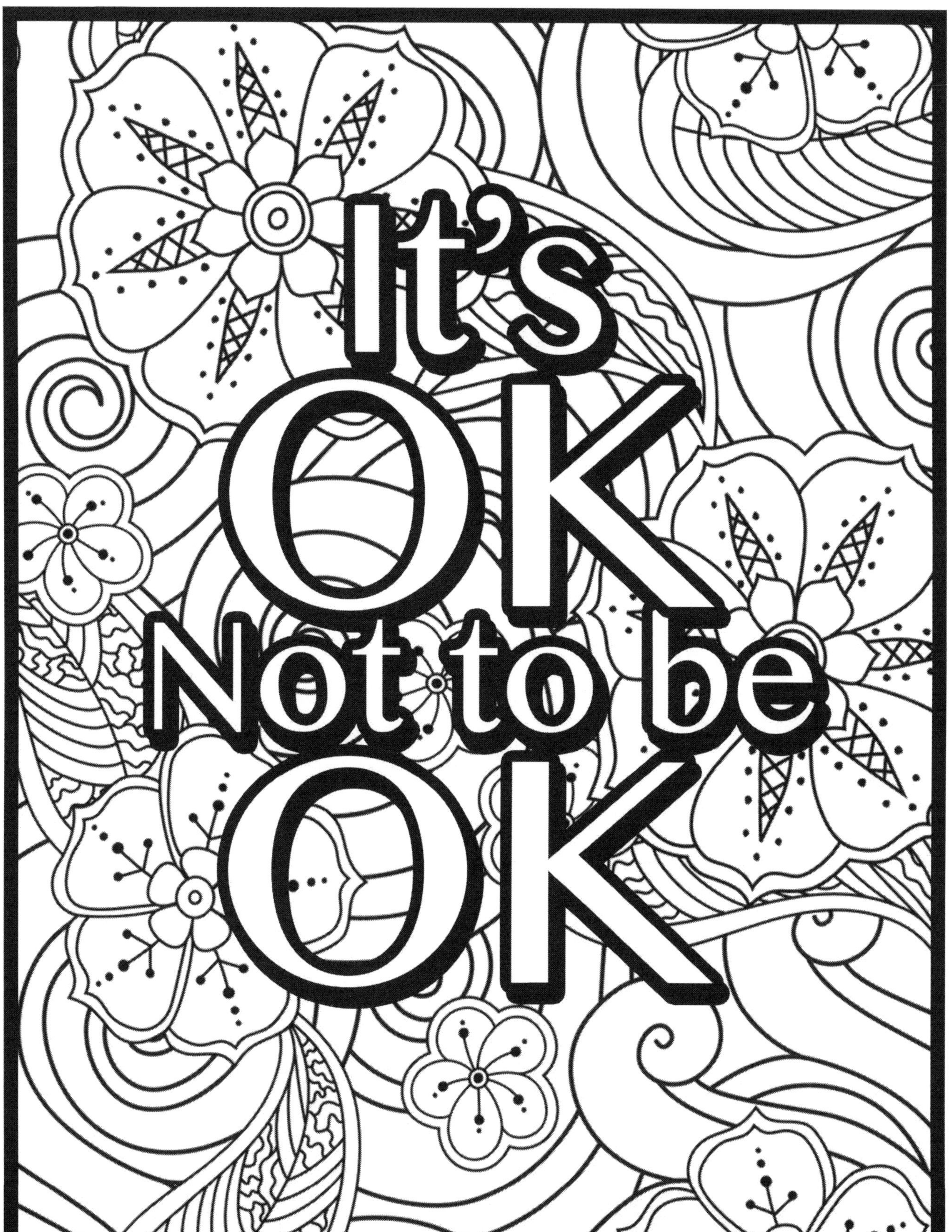
It's
OK
Not to be
OK

I Chose
the
Psycho
Path

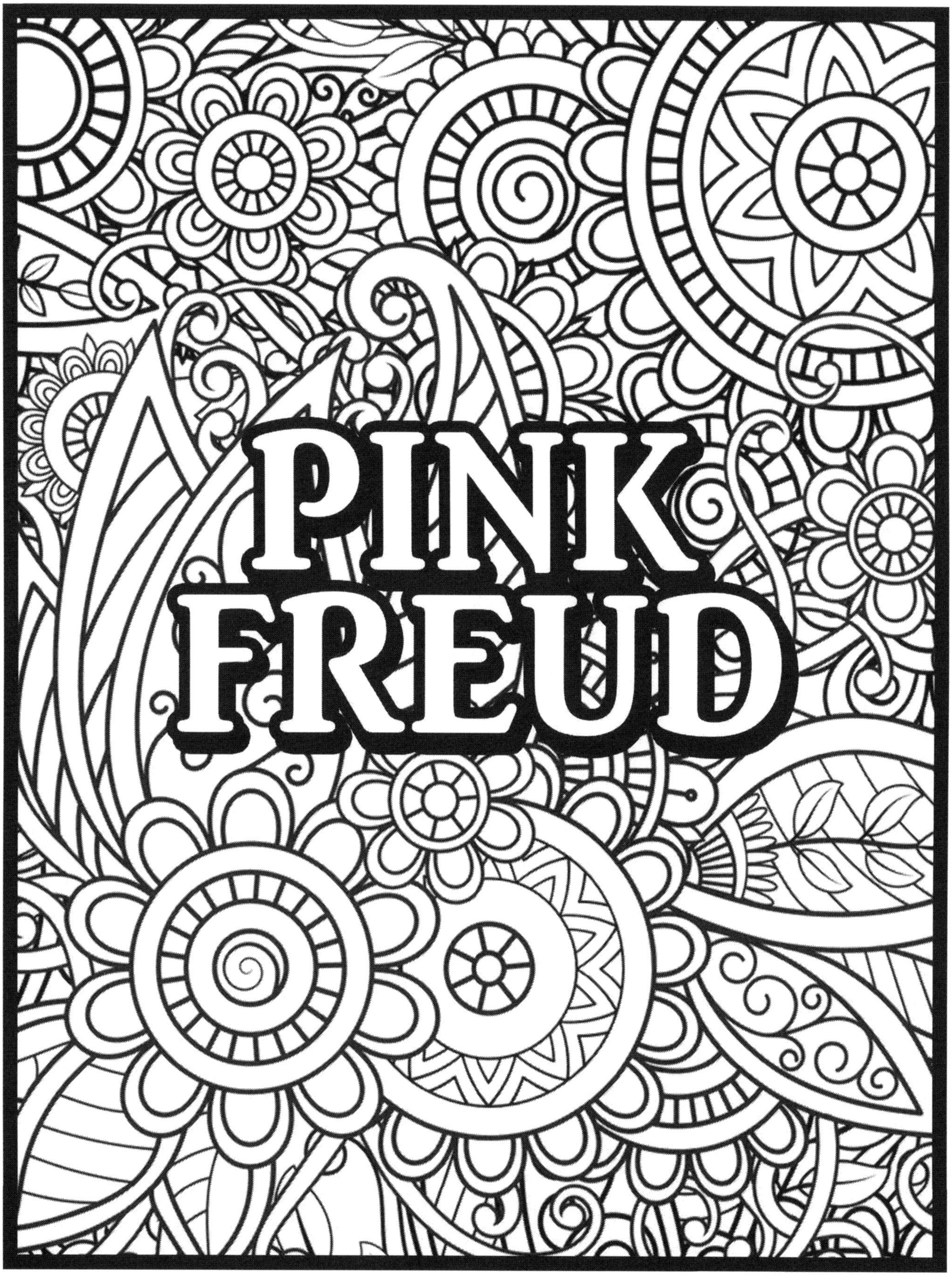
PINK
FREUD

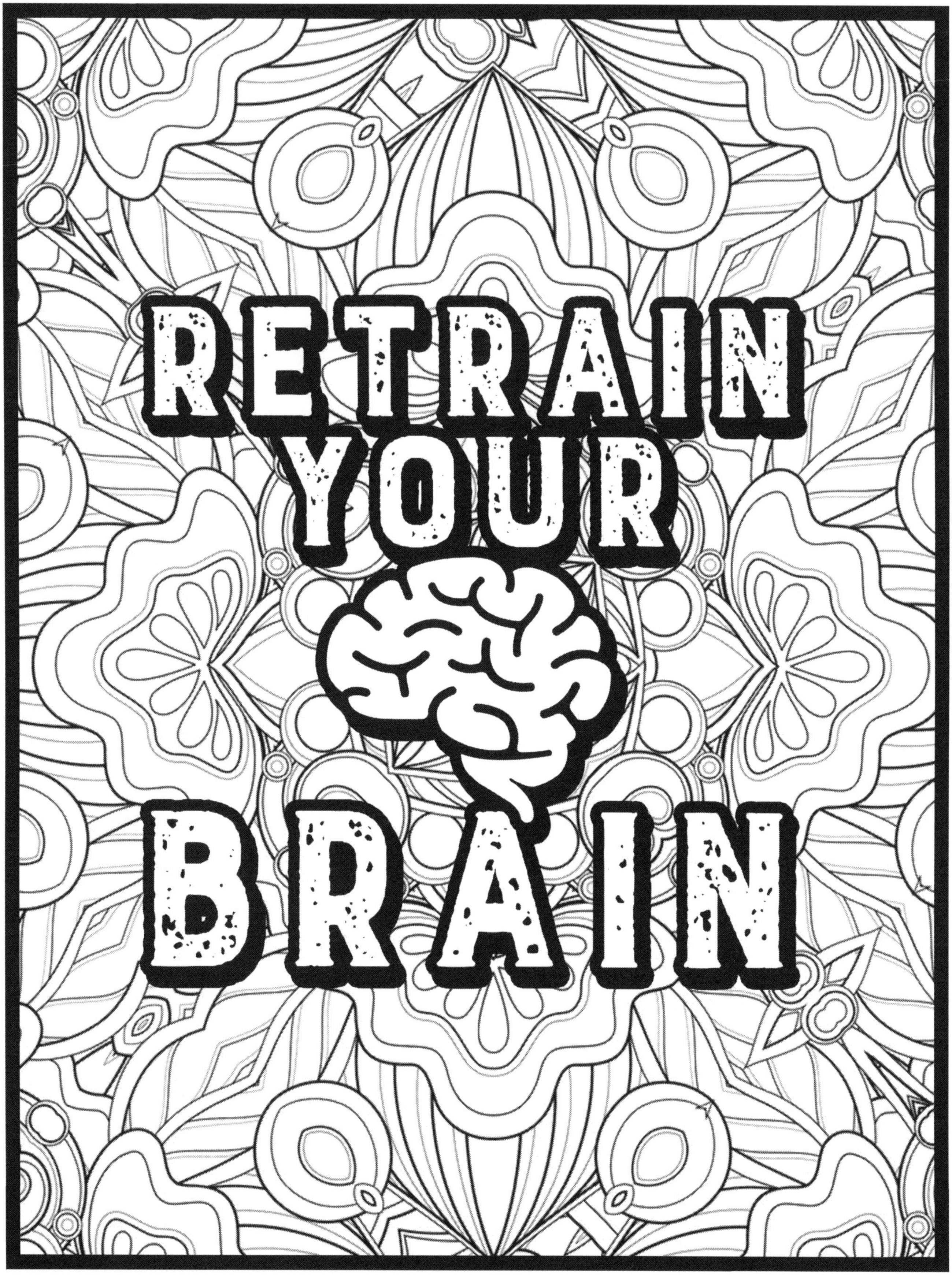
RETRAIN
YOUR
BRAIN

PSYCHOLOGY
I'M
ALLERGIC
TO STUPIDITY
I BREAK OUT IN
Sarcasm

I HAVE A
Psychology
DEGREE
OF COURSE YOU HAVE
Problems

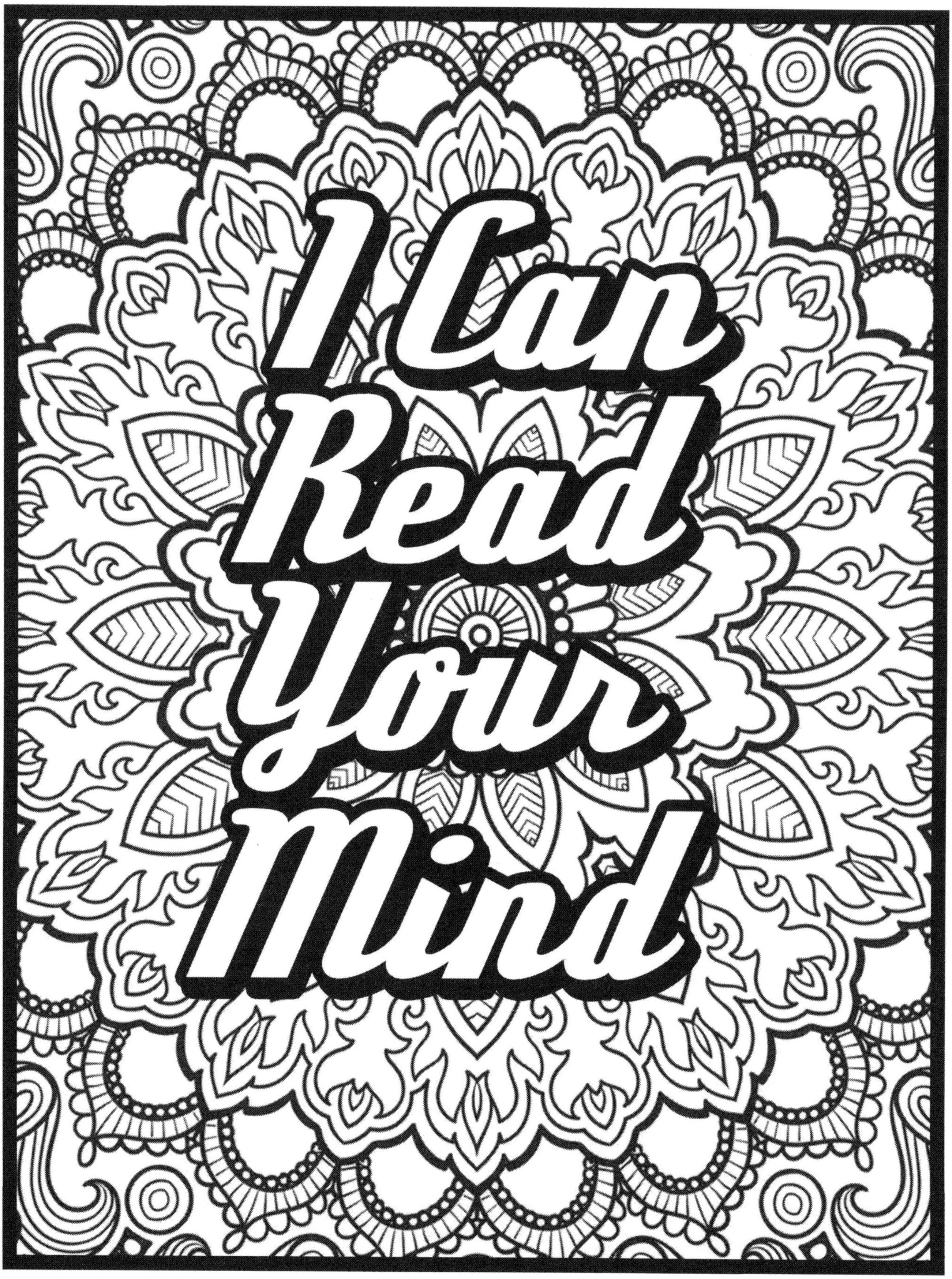
I Can Read Your Mind

I'M A
Psychiatrist
NOT A
Magician

I'M A
PSYCHIATRIST
WHAT'S YOUR
SUPER
POWER?

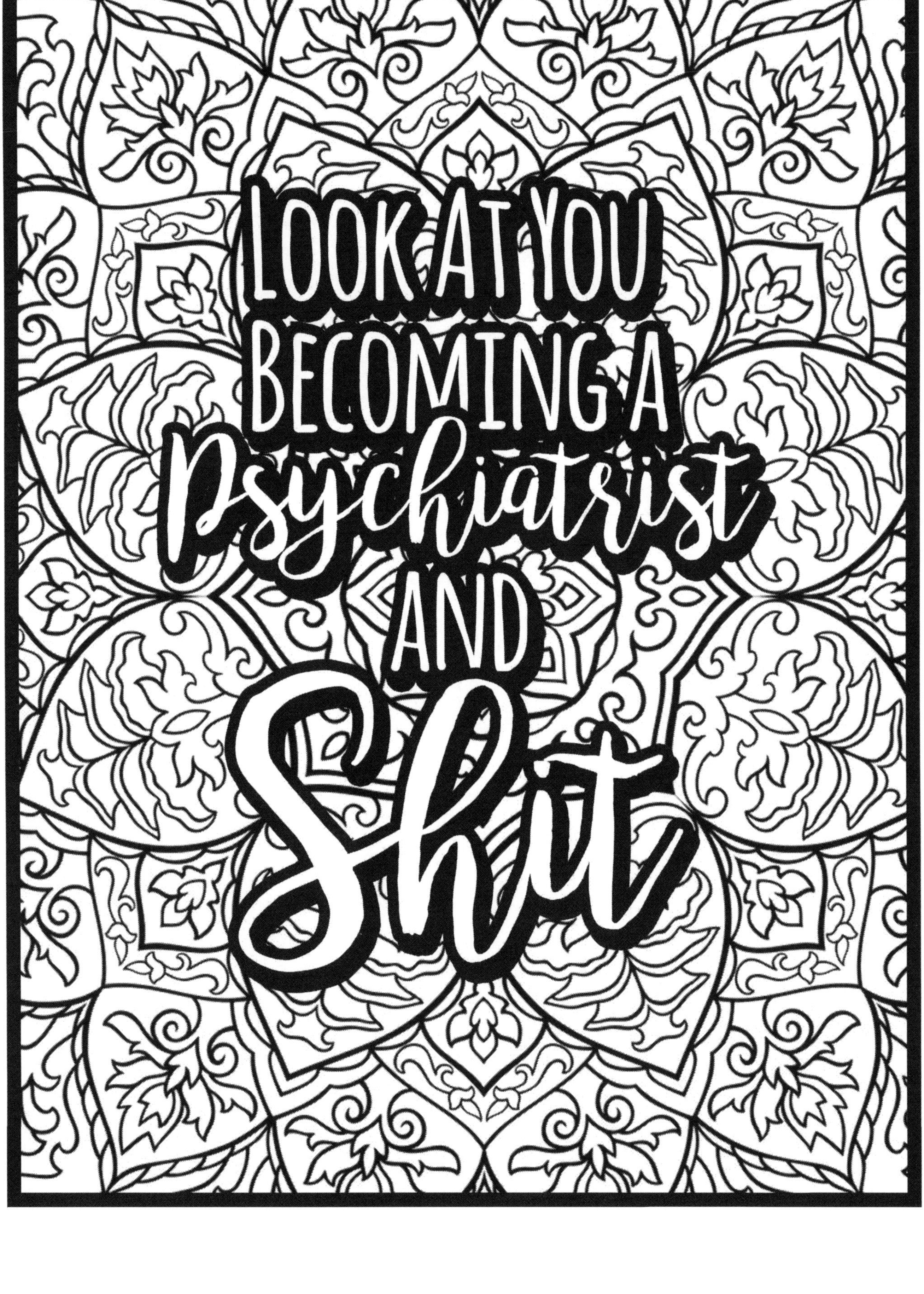
LOOK AT YOU
BECOMING A
Psychiatrist
AND
Shit

World's
BEST
Psychiatrist

Relax
WE'RE ALL
CRAZY!
IT'S NOT A
COMPETITION

Because
i'm the
psychiatrist
That's Why!

DON'T MAKE
ME USE MY
Psychiatrist
VOICE

THIS
Psychiatrist
NEEDS A
MOTHER
FUCKING
Nap!

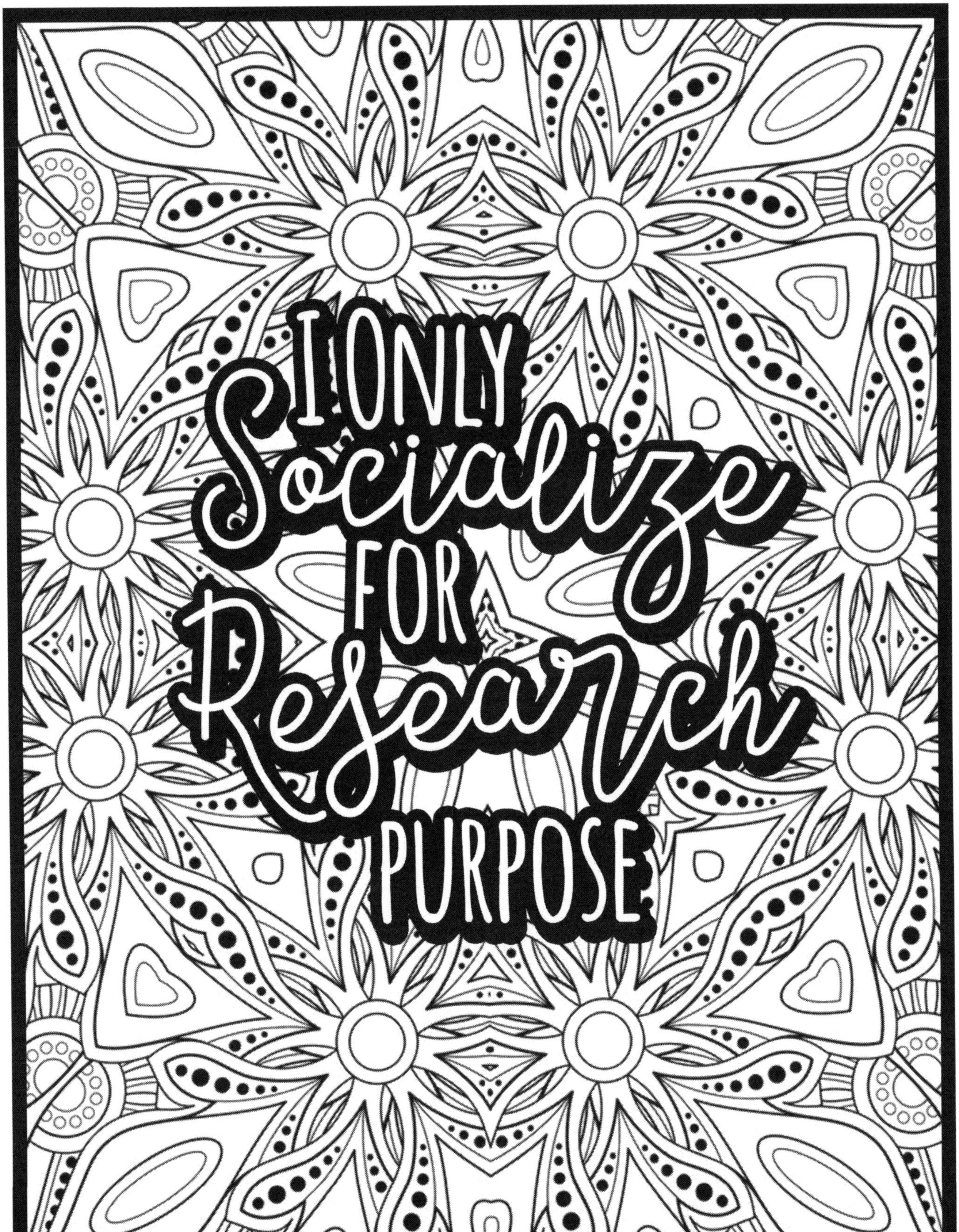
I ONLY
Socialize
FOR
Research
PURPOSE

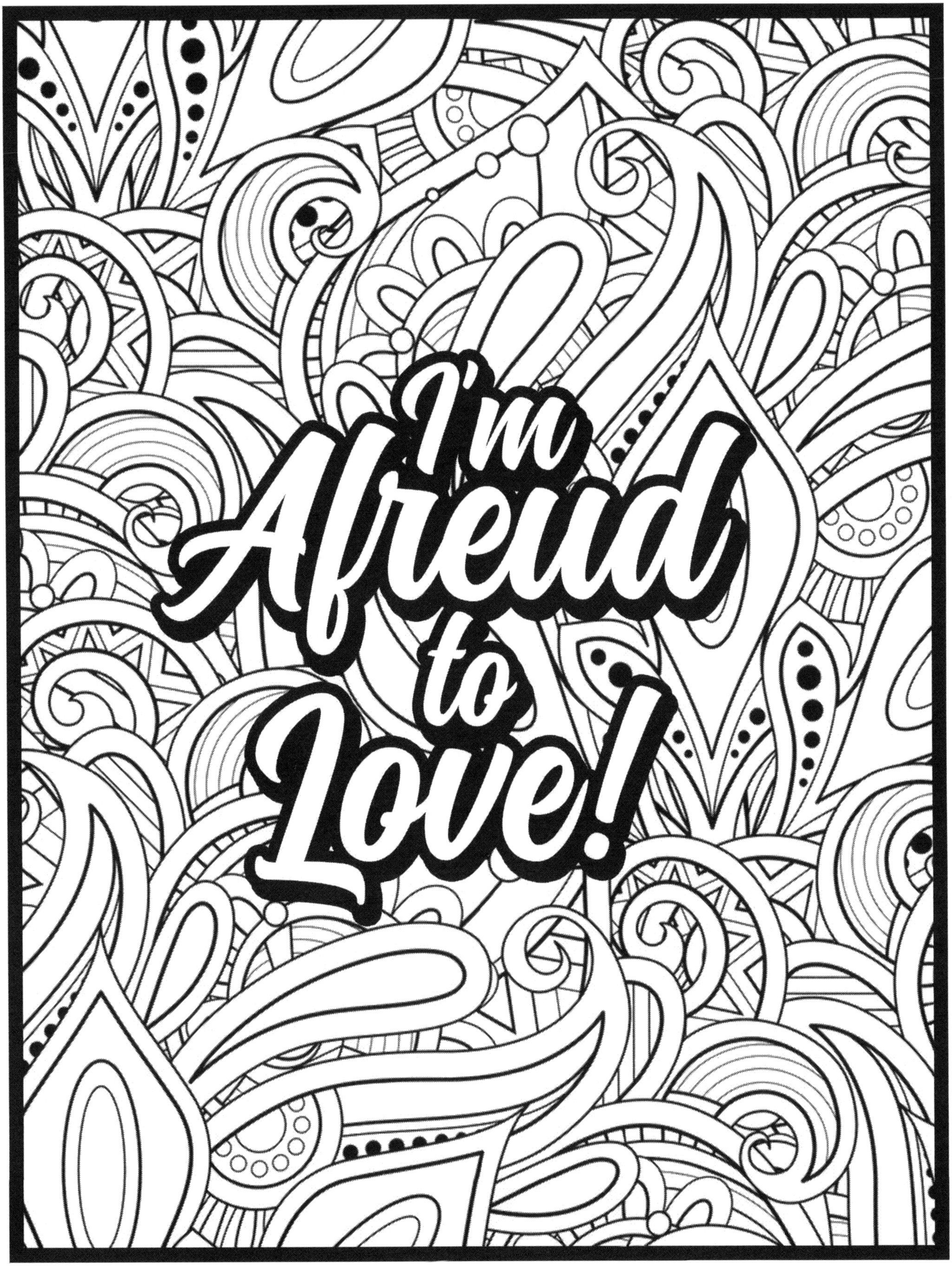
I'm Afreud to Love!

KEEP TALKING
I'M
Diagnosing
You

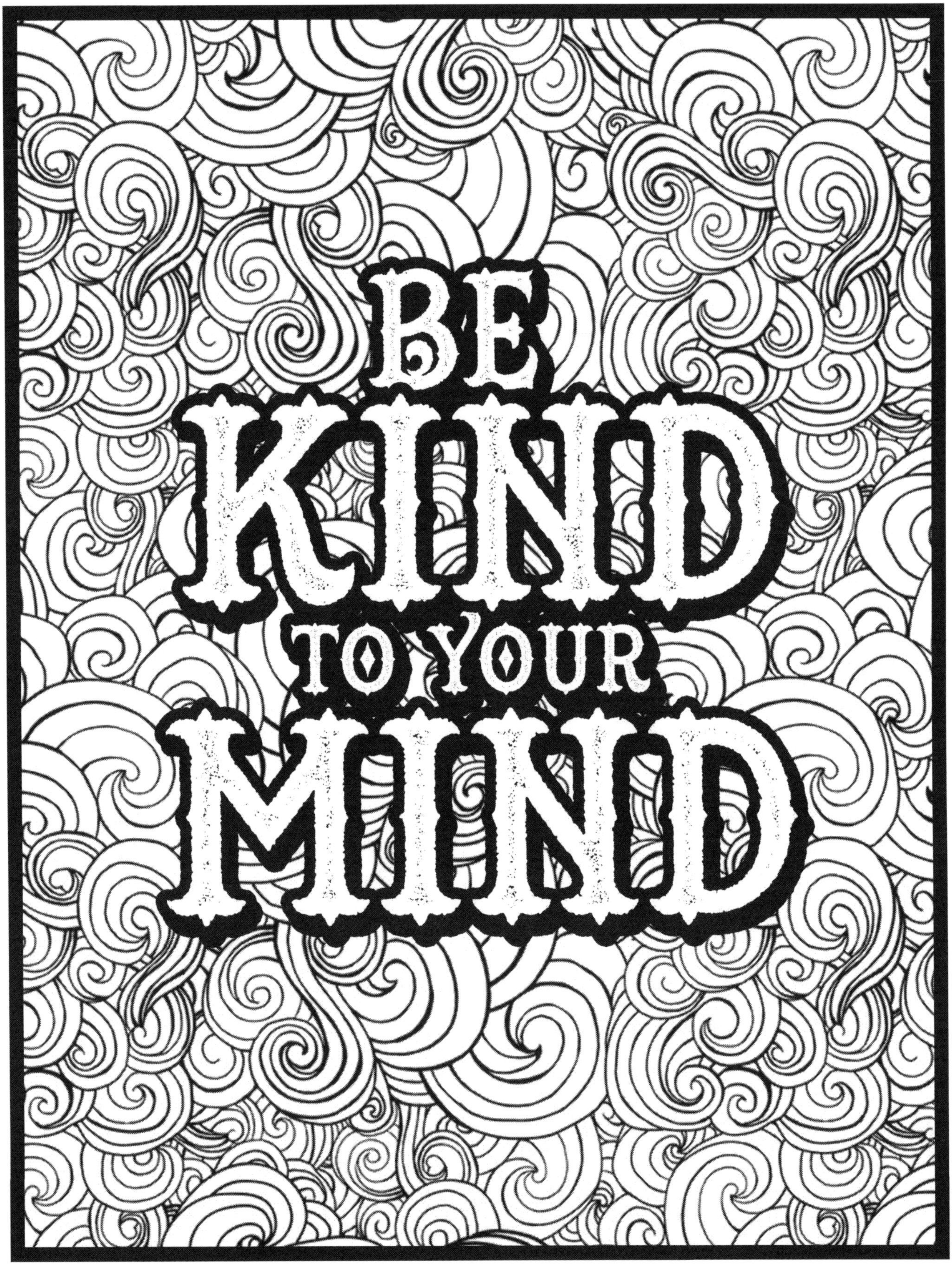
BE
KIND
TO YOUR
MIND

Printed in Great Britain
by Amazon

63382250R00025